To you who &

[handwritten]

SELF-APPRAISAL

Discovering & Maximising Your Potential

I wish you a Happy +
blessed New year!

VALMA JAMES
2024

This was my four edition
enjoy!

WOW Book Publishing™

SELF-APPRAISAL:
Discovering & Maximising Your Potential

Valma James

Copyright 2020 © Valma James

WOW Book Publishing

ISBN: 9781701797413

The purpose of this book is to educate and entertain. The views and opinions expressed in this book are that of the author based on her personal experiences and education. The author does not guarantee that anyone following the techniques, suggestions, ideas or strategies will become successful.

The author shall neither be liable nor responsible for any loss or damage allegedly arising from any information or suggestion in this book.

Dedication

To whomever reads this book, I wish you peace, harmony, love, and self-love!

Recognise that you were and have been created for a purpose — it is finding that purpose that creates your journey and gives you a new perspective on life. I wish you well in finding your purpose!

Table of contents

Table of contents

Self-Appraisal

Table of contents

Self-Appraisal

A Little Example

*My experience of how we might miss
the key aspects of our talents that
others will see.*

Who would have known that a stranger
knew I was destined for a career in radio before
I did.

In 2010, a stranger, to whom I spoke while I
ordered my printer ink cartridge asked me, "Do
you do radio?" I replied, "No." He replied that
I had a voice for radio. I took the compliment
light heartedly at the time.

A year later, the producers of AUKRADIO
came into my office where I provided training
and coaching to informal carers and the
unemployed,. They were looking for ideas for
radio shows, I suggested that radio should be
used as a mechanism for community education,
specifically concerning social, economic, and
health issues.

Self-Appraisal

I suggested the programme be called "Cultur'us". It was suggested that I come to the radio show; initially, the idea was crazy, as I had never been on a radio.

I was under the impression that they were going to interview me; however, when I turned up at the station, I was told that I was going to present. So I sat behind the micro-phone and put the headphones on my head. I never looked back, because I had spent so many years reaching out to individuals and families in the community to engage them in improving their economic situation and the importance of increasing their children's educational opportunities.

Through the use of radio, I recognised that it was the vehicle for sharing information, knowledge, and empowering communities that I call "planting the seed and promoting individual responsibility".

I now present on Hospital Radio Bedford and am member of Health Radio UK. What a transformation that was, completely unexpected. That's the thing; we never know what our journey will entail!

Dear Reader

I wrote this book because, for several years, I spent a lot of my time inspiring others to be the best that they can be through building their confidence, self-esteem, and facilitating contact with appropriate institutions and agencies so that they can offer more expert advice and information.

My overall aim is to encourage individuals to engage in personal development as a means of widening personal, social, and economic growth and identifying opportunities to further their advancement. They would accomplish this by identifying and exploring opportunities and creating the life they want. Writing this book has given me the means to share my philosophy and passion for human development.

Self-Appraisal

If you are an individual that lacks confidence, self-esteem, and allows procrastination to get in the way of your growth and true potential, I hope that this book will inspire you to recognise that your potential and capacity to succeed lies with you.

Continuously Self-Appraisal

By completing these steps, you will achieve your goal and create the life you want.

"Don't look at others before observing Yourself"

—Valma James,
Radio Presenter and Life Coach

Testimonials

Valma wrote this book because she wants to empower and inspire you to leverage your experience, knowledge, and expertise. You are personally responsible for your personal development and ultimately in control over your own destiny.

Because the manner in which you allow others to speak to you can affect your self-confidence and self-worth, Valma believes choosing the positive is the first step. Valma has developed her experience in coaching and networking though engaging in her own personal and professional development with a range of institutions, community organisations, and networking.

Valma has gained her experience in working with people over 30 years, using her capacity to think out of the box as a lateral and strategic thinker in her job as a nurse, social worker, youth worker, community development worker engaged in health and social care planning, commissioning and quality performance at a managerial level.

Valma was a volunteer life coach with Youth At Risk(Luton). Employed by Open University as a outreach community education worker. Was also employed by Luton University as a Senior University Lecturer and Evidence Based Practice Facilitator.

Currently she works as an independent Life Coach, author, radio broadcaster/presenter with AUKRADIO.COM and Hospital Radio Bedford. Org.uk

"You cannot be dependent on others to change you; it is ultimately your journey."

— **Vishal Morjaria**
Award Winning Author
& International Speaker

Testimonials

Valma has been inspiring in her journey and teaching. She has been supporting young people and adults in their discovery processes. Valma's book, *Self-Appraisal*, will encourage you to take action and challenge you to create more value within yourself. I recommend her as a 'go to' person to help with your reconnection of your true potential.

— Andrew CM Miller
Award Winning Author
& Transitional Coach

As National Carers Week 2019 approached (and as the government's recently published long-term plan on the future of the NHS and proposals for Universal Personal Care underline the importance of better support for the UK's 7.6 million carers), I am delighted to provide a testimonial for the work of Valma James.

As Vice-President of Carers UK and as the Chair of the Government's Standing Commission on Carers for six years, I am very aware of the need for more talented and committed leaders in the carers' sector, and I have long been impressed by Valma's energy, creativity, and her ongoing commitment to improving the lives of carers.

Valma James is a registered nurse and social worker with over twenty years' experience of working in the voluntary, statutory, and private sectors, developing a range of innovative support for carers, including Fresh Start (developing self-confidence and skills in carers to enable them to consider employment), support for carers of people in the mental health sector and using forensic services (an often forgotten community), and autism.

Valma has always been committed to collaborative leadership, actively involving carers as well as those they support, staff, managers and commissioners in thinking strategically about service design and championing integration.

Valma has had lead responsibilities within organisations for initiating and building partnership, developing consultation mechanism, including influencing government policies.

Valma's dynamic approach and wide personal professional expertise have enabled her to raise the profile of carers (at a local and national level) as expert partners in care. Her creativity is exemplified by the conference that she has organised for Carers Week on autism and new approaches to whole family support and, importantly, to collaborative solutions to some major challenges for carers.

The new expectations about better integration between health and social care and the emphasis on personalisation at every level need new (but experienced) voices to find the best way forward. Valma is and has always been both an innovator and a manager who understands that big ideas need sound systems to deliver them.

I feel that I personally have always learned a lot from Valma, and I have no doubt that her voice will become increasingly significant in a care sector where family carers are valued, supported, and seen as the citizens first as envisaged in the Care Act 2014 and the Government' 2018 Carers Action Plan.

— Dame Philippa Russell

I first met Valma some 12 years ago, when she was chairing a meeting for Senior Citizens' issues, at which she was most dedicated. Full of ideas and suggestions, she impressed me enormously. She worked, and still works tirelessly for other people, and she encouraged me to become the Chairman of this group. I must admit that I was not capable of succeeding her but tried my best until another successor came along. With Valma's assistance, this group developed into BEDSCARF — Bedfordshire Senior Citizens Art and Recreational Forum, whereby it was linked to International Older Persons' Day, the date recognised by European Associates as 1st October each year.

As I was very interested in music and producing shows, my company, the Happy Wanderers, became synonymous with BEDSCARF when, in October each year, we produced a series of events for International

Testimonials

Older Persons' Day. This included a concert by the Happy Wanderers variety group, of which I am pleased to say that Valma joined as a singer, and a good one at that. In that capacity, she has entertained at many residential homes, as well as the Carnival Arts Centre in Luton and the Barn Theatre, Welwyn Garden City.

A most dynamic and influential woman, Valma is never lost for a solution to most problems and manages to get the best out of everyone with whom she associates. Her efforts have had dramatic effects on those she encounters, and I am very proud to have known and worked with her.

—Harry Rappaport
Musical Composer: Happy Wanderers

About the Author

Valma is a qualified registered nurse and social worker. She practices as a health and social care consultant, life coach and radio presenter with AUKRadio and Hospital Radio Bedford. Valma has developed her knowledge, expertise and experience within the NHS, public sector, private sector, and community development.

Through applying strategic, innovative, creative, and imaginative thinking to solve problems and find appropriate solutions that improve the quality of services to consumers, she is passionate about and committed to improving peoples' lives.

Valma has worked with numerous groups, young people, older people, the Lesbian, Gay, Bisexual and Transgender (LGBT+ community, women, children, disabled, and even whole families. She has also held managerial positions that primarily addressed quality assurance, performance management, diversity and equalities, reviewing policies, developing and commissioning services and project management of community projects.

Valma has had lead responsibilities within organisations for initiating and building partnerships, developing consultation mechanisms, and influencing government policies.

An example of her work includes implementing Ethnic Monitoring within GP practices, the integration of the needs of family carers within NHS hospital discharge policy framework, initiating carers health and welling centre, developing community-based care support services for ethnic minorities, health educational screening programmes, supported in developing Luton, Dunstable Sickle Cell, and Thalassaemia services, including the training of medical and clinical staff and creating innovative projects to address social inclusion and health and socialcare inequalities, most importantly working with health and local authorities to improve the engagement of consumers in local authority consultation processes to improve better service outcomes.

Valma was the first to establish the Grahame Park Balley School for deprived children through negotiating collaboration with the Royal College of Ballet, organised the first young women's personal development programme, and organized the first Youth Council.

Whilst working with Bedfordshire Health Authority and under the leadership of Dr. Woolway, Director of Public Health, Valma received a commendation from Dr. John Reid, Secretary of Health and Chief Medical Officer (DOH) 1999, for her work with ethnic minorities. She has always taken responsibility for her own professional and personal development and has strived to improve her own performance, capabilities, and potential.

Valma has never stopped thinking and exploring new ways to help others achieve their true potential, always seeking transformation though self-empowerment.

—Dame Phillipa Russell

Foreword

It is an honour to be asked to write the foreword for Valma's book *Self-Appraisal*, which is a book that will encourage individuals to recognise that it is possible to grow their own potential and create the life they want.

I have personally taken an interest in supporting Valma in publishing her book, because she has been engaged in helping so many others in developing their potential, confidence, and career through sharing her own expertise, experience and encouraging the pursuit of promoting professional and self-development.

In this book, the author covers the importance of self-appraisal and personal empowerment to achieve your professional goals, hopes, and dreams. This is without depending on someone else telling you your self-worth, what your value is to an organization, and whether you're "good enough".

For some, the main interest in reading this book will be about integrating positive self- talk as part of making communication good for your psychological and emotional wellbeing. Doing so will allow you to achieve your professional and personal goals and take control of your destiny and future.

The book demonstrates why positioning yourself for your next career promotion is your business and responsibility—whether it be remaining in an organisation or seeking to establish your own consultancy.

So, whatever your particular role, whether it be in the public, private, or voluntary sector, and you want to take the next step into your career, this book will certainly be a catalyst for your personal and professional development.

—Vishal Morjaria
award winning author
and international speaker

Acknowledgement

I would like to acknowledge those who have influenced the person that I am today and those who have been part of my journey. My mother, Elizabeth Brotherson, my uncle Zacharia Brotherson, and Gertrude Brotherson.

My teacher, Mrs. Porter, who had every faith in me as a pupil and taught me how to be a young woman at the Nansen Girls School. An American teacher, who attended an American finishing school, she showed me the principles of etiquette and social graces. I have since passed these skills onto my children and others.

Another teacher, Mrs. Griffiths, who was my music teacher, exposed me to classical music and opera, which I still love to this day, and engaged me in the school choir. My thanks to Harry Rappaport, local composer in Luton, for encouraging me to join his group, Happy

Self-Appraisal

Wanderers, and had the most pleasurable and amazing experience singing to the elderly in residential homes.

Tony Robbins, by attending his programme "Unleash the Power Within" Excel 2017, transformed my life, and he is still transforming my life every day.

Oprah Winfrey and her enormous power to inspire people, Barrack Obama and Nelson Mandela, who demonstrated that the world can change and that we all have a purpose. Les Brown, a motivational coach who inspires others to realise that they, too, have the potential irrespective of their labels. Vishal Morjaria, awarding winning author.

Theresa May, who took the challenge in asking employers to monitor sex and race discrimination in the workplace and demonstrated "the staying power in her leadership", Her Royal Majesty the Queen, who acknowledged that a change has come by supporting the union of Harry and Megan.

Shirley Bassey and Aretha Franklin, who demonstrated that voice can travel to your

Acknowledgement

soul. Mirela Sula, director of Global Women, who empowers women to have their voices heard. Martin Luther King, who demonstrated that vision and resilience are the prerequisite for change mastery.

Mahatma Gandhi, who proved that "not everyone can be fooled". Bill Gates, Dr. Hissah Saad, and A. Al-Sabah (Kuwait Princess) who have also demonstrated that wealth has a purpose in changing humanity. Dame Phillipa Russell for her support in helping me raise the profile of Family Carers and for recognising my work.

Feroze Dada, who has taught me the wisdom and principles of meditation and Peter Norrington, who made me realise that I can succeed instead of fail. My beautiful children, Becki and Abi, and my grandchildren, Celeste and Araya, and , last but not least, Keith Brotherson, who made the publishing this book possible.

I am truly grateful to have the "Divine" in life, and the abundance of love for humanity and the chosen path that have been created for me. I will continue to serve and be passionate in caring for those who have no voice or whose voice is not listened to.

A special thank you to Abi, my son for the amasing cover design, you can see more of Abi's work by having a look at this link, www.moworks.tv and thanks to Pauline Barath for overindulging time, and support.

Love suffers long and is kind ; love does not envy; love does not parade itself, is not puffed up; does not behave rudely, does not seek its own, is not provoked, thinks no evil, does not rejoice in iniquity, but rejoices in the truth, bears all, things, believes all things hopes all things endures all things . Love never fails. And now abide, faith, hope, love, of these three, the greatest of these is love.

—1 Corinthians 13:13

Love is truly an amazing thing!

XXX

For the Reader

The contents of the book are the personal views of the author, based on her experiences in an effort to improve her performance, potential, knowledge, experience, and skills. This book serves as an informational guide only and is not guaranteed for content accuracy or any other implied or explicit purpose. It is simply a tool that you can use to support you with growing your own potential.

What will you get from reading this book?

The book aims to engage you in several thought-provoking activities. The best way to read this book is to have an open mind and the capacity to take an in-depth critical overview of self, such as self-exploration self-reflection, and self-examination on what you want to achieve or intend to achieve with your accumulation of skills, knowledge, experience, training, and expertise acquired from being of service to others.

What actually motivated you to want to be of service to others? What does it tell you about yourself and your family, work colleagues, friends, employers, and people with which you have direct contact? How does it influence your interactions with clients, meeting individuals at training, social, and networking events?

This book will also provide insight into how you can make appraisal work for you, rather than the organisation making appraisal work for them. It will also show you how to monetise your talents, create the right mindset, let go of self-talk through developing and creating the right mental state and energy level, and allowing you to break free of your limitations by staying optimistic and growing your potential with confidence and integrity.

This book will also help you recognise that the first person who should be appraising you is, in fact, you most definitely for your appraisal with your manager or for an upcoming interview or to monitor your progress on a regular basis.

Hence, develop the skills and attributes necessary to ensure that you are first to appraise you by taking time to critically evaluate your self-worth, financially, personally, and professionally and transform and aspire to the next level of your personal development. Through utilising the accumulation of knowledge, experience, expertise, education, skills, and social contacts to serve your best interest. This progress is solely about you and how you can maximise your capabilities to enhance your quality of life, create the life you want, and feel fulfilled.

I have purposely called this process Your Self-Appraisal Tool Kit, a mechanism for maximizing your personal and professional development and your ability to continue to love serving others and creating a purpose in your life and for others.

We, as professionals, often get so engrossed in following organisational policies, procedure, and legal frameworks that we forget the reason why we entered the job in the first place and who and why we are serving; the clients get lost in the process. We forget the humanitarian aspect of the service, the capacity to rethink if we are doing the right thing for this person and the overall impact. In some cases, we have to consider the best interest of the person we are trying to serve. These are associated with numerous complexities, but are they soluble and can we be more creative?

We get a job, start with enthusiasm, build motivation, and, subsequently, we can reach to a point that when we arrive at work it is primarily to get paid and pay the bills. When the enthusiasm and love to work goes away, the light becomes darkness; it leads to a feeling of hopelessness and of being stuck in a rut. This, in turn, affects your self-confidence, self-esteem, performance, quality of life, customer care, customer relationship, and communication with those who we are there to serve. Why is it essential that you review whether you are serving your purpose?

"He or she who looks will find!"

—Valma James

Chapter 1

Self-Appraisal

Self-Appraisal Notes

_____

_____

_____

_____

_____

_____

_____

_____

_____

_____

_____

_____

_____

_____

_____

1. What is Self-Appraisal

Self-appraisal is examining oneself by reflecting on thoughts, attitude, and behaviour. It is your experiences, relationships with others, spirituality, career, social life, and identity, which serve as foundations to identify factors that either get in the way of your progress or your potential growth.

It is the ability to learn from experience in order to truly identify where you are and where your life is heading. Self-appraisal is also finished or unfinished journeys. When reflecting and self-appraising, your journey can also help you to remove those hidden barriers that have got in the way of your self- fulfilment and in creating the life you want.

2. Appraisal within Organisations

Organisations use appraisal for identifying the training needs of employees, by monitoring their performance and capabilities and planning the organisation's future. They develop new organisational structures, work programmes, access funding, policy, and legislative frameworks, new customers, as well as set and monitor targets. Grote (2002) argued that appraisal is perceived as a negative annual event where the supervisor or manager facilitates the whole process.

However, the process of organisational appraisal includes the evaluation of the quality of an individual's performance, by a supervisor or manager, and can be used to identify whether an employee is still suited to the needs of the organisation.

Some individuals may argue that appraisal is an instrument to weed out individuals that the organisation may want to get rid of. Obviously, no organisation is going to tell you that!

But you can feel the signs when you are excluded from meetings, work is allocated to someone else, when you are isolated and ignored, you do not engage in any meaningful conversation, and you suddenly find that your role is being or has been basically annulled.

In fact, they can make your life pretty miserable and uncomfortable, which then puts you in a state of survival mode or complete relapse and stress, seeing existence as failure. This causes fear, specifically fear of rejection, and, eventually, leads to depression, long-term sick leave, possible removal from the organisation by a pay-out, or long-term disabled sickness benefit due to mental health, including a period of having to either be on state benefits or utilise your financial savings. All of these cause extreme stress and impact on your self-confidence, self-esteem, family life, and quality of life. This is why taking control of your own self-appraisal allows you to make decisions about your future, not someone else making that decision for you — always be self-prepared.

Good organisations would help such individuals by offering personal development training such as job-hunting skills to help find alternative employment or alternative employment in another department; however, this has to be negotiated!

Self-Appraisal

Over many years, I have observed the process of organisational restructuring, the subsequent panic and anxiety caused among employees, not knowing if they still have a job or having to re-apply for their own jobs. Ultimately, this affects the staff morale, work environment, culture of the organisations and, more significantly, employees' inter-relationships. Eventually, it boils down to deterioration of the physical, emotional, and psychological well-being of employees and instigating stress and sickness absence.

An organisation's chief aim is to identify the needs of the organisation and maintain sustainability at whatever cost. We have seen numerous cases on the news showing people packing their boxes with their belongings when public and corporate businesses decide to make cuts in order to streamline their budget. Some employees are directly asked to leave by taking redundancy pay or find that their job/position has been made redundant or downgraded. Hence, there is very little concern on the impact of employees, but unfortunately, this is the society we have come to know. Some people survive and others do not! The term most commonly used is, "The survival of the fittest".

"It doesn't matter where you are,
you are nowhere compared to where
you can go."—Bob Proctor

3. Taking Responsibility for your Appraisal

Not all employees necessarily embrace appraisal, as some find it very threatening; others see it as an opportunity to appraise their position and an opportunity for promotion, which is very seldom. Some argue using the expression of "if your face fit, you're OK Jack ".

Therefore, my view is that staff have to continuously do their own self-appraisal and not wait for the organisation to appraise them. It is too late, as you will not be in control of your own destiny.

Why wait for someone to appraise you, like a supervisor or manager, so that they can inform you of your worth to the organisation?

Self-Appraisal

Why not you, as an individual or employee, use the same process of appraisal to monitor your own performance and identify your worth to the organisation, rather than someone else telling you your worth to them — as ironic it may seem, it is the reality.

Why not self-appraise your skills, knowledge, experience, expertise, talents, and capabilities so that you are in a prime and powerful position to negotiate your value to the organization, which can enhance your sustainability or potential to move on to newer grounds. Why not leverage your years of experience? Don't you want to take responsibility for your personal growth and be in control for a change?

Why give your power away to the organisation and the power for them to decide your worth!? Allowing this to happen is perhaps the most destructive process for killing one's confidence, self-esteem, self-worth, and integrity.

Thinking of this makes me reflect on the history of the Industrial Revolution and Karl Marx's theory regarding the class structure in

British Society. In his theory, he argues that a capitalist society consists of two main classes:

1. The bourgeoise, whom he defines as the capitalist who has the means of production.

2. The proletariat—the working class who must sell their own power of labour. Reflecting on Marx's theory, it could be argued still remains the status quo—and will continue if employees fail to recognise and place a value on their worth to the organisation and system.

4. Why you need to prepare for your Appraisal

Just imagine the wealth of knowledge, skills, expertise, and experience that you have accumulated over the years. You have gained all these credentials from all the places you have worked, where you had access to training, in-house training, or access to an external educational institution in which you gained recognised qualifications. No doubt the training attending college or university or being allocated a mentor or a coach. In the current economic climate, formal training such as leave to attend college or university and the organisation paying for the course is not so easily accessible and is a privilege to many employees.

"Don't say you don't have enough time. You have exactly the same number of hours per day that were given to Helen Keller, Pasteur, Michaelangelo, Mother Teresea, Leonardo da Vinci, Thomas Jefferson, and Albert Einstein."
—*Life's Little Instruction Book*

Chapter 2

Empowerment and Disempowerment

Empowerment and Disempowerment Notes

_____

_____

_____

_____

_____

_____

_____

_____

_____

_____

_____

_____

_____

_____

1. Recognising Empowerment and Disempowerment

Have you ever had a manager that has called you into his or her office in such a way that you feel that you are back at school or in kindergarten? The manner in which they communicate can indicate their attitude towards you, whether they like or dislike you and have your best interest at heart. For some managers, it could be argued as an opportunity to bring you down a peg or two, using it to humiliate or undermine you.

In these circumstances, what have you done to halt their disempowerment? Reflect on an experience on where this has happened to you and how it made you feel. Then reflect on an experience when the manager was communicating to you in a positive way and offering constructive criticism; how did you feel then? There is a difference in your emotions, and you can feel it within your energy zone.

This is all about the mental state that you are in and why you need to be a positive state to lessen the emotional damage and impact on your self-confidence and self-esteem. This is also related to your relationship with those in power and how their communication style can either disempower or empower you (in the form of anxiety, panic attacks, and stress every time you hear their voice or in contact with them).

> **"By changing nothing, nothing changes."—Tony Robbins**

2. A Story

Anne was a manager and was responsible for a board that included senior directors and middle managers. Anne was asked to do a presentation by the head of the department on an area that she was not familiar with. However, she made every effort to research the relevant information on the subject to do the presentation. During supervision, Anne's manager informed her that she did not have the credentials to do the presentation, as it was not her area of expertise.

What would you have done in this situation?

3. Creating the Right State of Mind

Being in control of your emotions and taking responsibility for your emotions puts you in control. However, you have to be prepared to put yourself in the right state of mind feeling empowered rather than feeling disempowered.

Your body language and voice can determine your mental state and your vulnerability. For example, when you are feeling low, your voice changes to a lower pitch, and your energy level is also low. Your communication becomes lethargic with no substance, which affects your mental state and can determine your recovery from the situation, either positively or negatively, and has a direct impact on your confidence and self-esteem. So having the right mental state is important to your survival!

Research has shown how positivity can affect your mental state and is reported to enhance physical and mental recovery as well as speed up your recovery.

If you are walking into a manager's office in a negative state, you are bound to spiral down and leave the office completely disempowered. However, if you create a positive mental state before entering the office, you are in a better position to deal and cope with the situation.

Do you agree that your state of mind, for example feeling negative or positive, can affect your interaction and your outcome? You don't have to be a psychologist or study psychology to recognise that your energy levels has a strong correlation with how you interact with others.

4. Self-Regulation

How can you self-regulate your emotions so that you maintain a high level of energy, self-confidence, self-esteem, and self-worth? Meditation and mindfulness are a good approach to getting rid of negative energy. You can find a quiet place to calm the mind so that the negative vibes in the office do not overwhelm you. If it is a possibility at your place of employment, excuse yourself for a few minutes, get some fresh air, create the mental state that you want.

Empowerment and Disempowerment

Story 2: Jane was employed as a researcher, and her manager was responsible for four other staff members, one of whom was a junior administrator, Pauline. Jane had asked her manager if she could attend an MBA course as part of her personal development as she wanted to apply for a more senior management position in the future. Her manager informed her that she had enough qualifications and did not need more. However, Jane decided to take the course anyway by financing it herself.

A new position had opened in the team for a senior role that Jane was not made aware of. She subsequently found out that Pauline, the junior administrator, was offered the position and was promoted over her.

How would you have handled the situation?

The only person better than you is the one you allow to think that they are better than you!

Create the energy that will bring out the best in you and the affirmation that will drive you to your goal—don't ponder on anyone else energy—but your own!

Self-Appraisal

**People will or can try and do to you
what they may not do to themselves—
cause pain or discomfort. It only
reflects on how they feel about self.
Remember, sticks and stones
may hurt my bones—but words
will never sink me!**

—Valma

*No one can make you feel inferior
without your consent."*
—Eleanor Roosevelt, *This is My Story*

Chapter 3

Recognising Your Value

Recognising Your Value Notes

_____

_____

_____

_____

_____

_____

_____

_____

_____

_____

_____

_____

_____

_____

1. Recognising Your Value

One of the most important factors of self-appraisal is that it can motivate you to examine every aspect of yourself, career, education, social life, emotional, physiological, psychological, and financial state as well as your relationships with others. It can even change the way you communicate.

Recognising and knowing your true value plays a significant role in where you perceive your level of fulfilment and self-satisfaction, including your perception of self-belief.

When self-appraising, you must be very frank and self-critical, and you need to take the knocks and the bumps, even if it makes you feel uncomfortable about what you are observing about yourself. You may find it useful to engage a professional coach to support you in identifying your values and how your values contribute to self-satisfaction. Getting feedback is always useful in understanding how others perceive you — it may be painful to hear, but you can learn from it!

Self-Appraisal

Time to Think!

- What are your Values?

  _____

  _____

- Do your values link with you work ethics and Passion?

  _____

  _____

  _____

- How do your Values contribute to your Character? What were the emotions you experienced?

  _____

  _____

  _____

- Are your Values in line with your Beliefs?

  _____

  _____

2. Self Confidence

Recognising traits about your characteristics, you can choose to do something about it. This includes changing your behaviour to what will serve you best. Fundamentally, knowing yourself will put you in a better position to take control and responsibility for your future.

Your level of confidence and self-esteem is all interlinked with your values and beliefs. However, some individuals feel extremely uncomfortable with expressing self-confidence. There are individuals who resent individuals who are confident, to the fact that some may even wish their downfall and may conspire or purposely create a situation to bring them down a peg or two or attempt to keep them in their place.

Unfortunately, people who lack confidence and self-esteem feel bad about themselves and their circumstances and often attempt to bring other confident people down to their own energy level.

They do so by communicating negatively towards you, never complimenting you, always criticising or finding faults, including getting others to support their perception of you to the extent of making you feel isolated and alienated. You often wonder whether these individuals have a life of their own, or are so unhappy that they bring others down because they feel bad about themselves. Maybe it is their own deeper problems or issues, and they do not realise how their energy affects others — sometimes it may be best to observe!

Maintaining your positive energy levels, being true to your values and self-belief, and building your resilience is the most appropriate approach for dealing and managing the negative energy that may enter into your energy zone. It is almost like having a balloon around you that allows negative energy to bounce off and prevent contamination.

"Never, never, never, never give up."
—Winston Churchill

3. How the Work Environment Can Impact Your Internal Energy

The office gossiper can create negativity in the environment, their energy level is low and the environment is perceived as uncomfortable. Negative energy impacts and disrupts the calmness of the environment.

You can walk into the office and literally feel the negative vibes and hostility; being exposed to such negative environment can make you want to leave immediately, become isolated, and either switch off or find an escape route.

Other factors that can negatively affect organisational environment and alter the energy level in an organisation are when a group of people sticks together and keeps you out of their group. Such groups can become powerful, because they can assert influence and are often referred to as the "In-Group". Some members of these groups have access to information, access to senior managers, have the ability to influence other people, and can make you feel excluded.

Self-Appraisal

At work, we cannot necessarily choose who we work with or who we are teamed up with. However, we do have control and choice over who we engage with after work and who we have in our lives. It could be argued that our work environment is just as important as the external environment because, think about it, spending up to eight or twelve hours a day with people you like or don't like is bound to rub off their attitude and behaviour on you.

Unhealthy environments. Some may argue that office gossip is another way of finding out what's going on in the organisation and with other people. However, the process can seemingly either alienate or isolate other people and cause unnecessary grief, stress, and anxiety.

- Have you ever experienced this situation?

_____

_____

- How did it make you feel?

_____

_____

Recognising Your Value

- What were the emotions you experienced?

  _____

  _____

- What was the environment like for you?

  _____

  _____

- What was your response?

  _____

  _____

- Having reflected and self-appraised your response, what would, or could you have done differently?

  _____

  _____

"Judge not, that you be not judged. "For with judgment you judge, you will be judged and with the measurers you use, it will measured back to you. And why do you look at the speck in

your brother's eye, but do not consider the plank in your own eye?

Hypocrite! First remove the plank from your own eye and then you will see clearly to remove the speck from your brother's eye".

—**Matthew 6:21**

"Whoever guards his month and tongue
Keeps his soul from troubles"
—**Proverbs 20:23**

4. Story: Critical Self

Linda was referred to human resources as she was experiencing high levels of anxiety associated with the uncertainty of her current employment. Her current position was going to be made obsolete within the organisational structure. She was offered other positions but was not interested because she perceived she did not have the necessary skills, knowledge, and experience for the roles offered to her.

It shook her self-confidence and self-esteem and also had an effect on her social and family life. Linda was offered counselling and therapeutic mindfulness relaxation techniques to deal with her panic and anxiety attacks.

A coach was allocated to Linda to help redevelop her self-confidence and self- esteem.

Linda then undertook self-appraisal to identify what type of career path and job she would be more suited to and was in line with her passion. Linda was assisted in compiling a new CV and interviewing skills and was successful in gaining a job that matched her skills, experience, expertise, and knowledge and had the capacity to grow and develop her new role.

Obviously, when you are self-appraising yourselves, you need to be prepared to be brutally critical, even to the extent of identifying and recognising behaviours in you that you really don't want to accept. However, it is only when you acknowledge all your strengths and weaknesses that you can really start to transform, because then you have nothing to hide from yourself or others. You become a better person spiritually, Psychologically, and emotionally as you observe your transformation.

You learn to free your soul and mind, until, eventually, that negative energy and fear gradually fade away, leaving you with a sense of utter psychological and emotional freedom and unselfish self-love.

When you leave no place for hate to fester within you, the abundance of love available to you from the Divine sets you free and allows you to love yourself and others even more.

- What are the things that you perceive are keeping you back from achieving your true potential? List them!

_____

_____

_____

_____

_____

_____

Recognising Your Value

- What actions are you going to take to rid yourself of negative self-talk?

  _____

  _____

  _____

  _____

- What methods will you use to sustain a high level of energy?

  _____

  _____

  _____

  _____

- What would you do each day to self-regenerate?

  _____

  _____

  _____

  _____

Self-Appraisal

Notes

_____

_____

_____

_____

_____

_____

_____

_____

_____

_____

_____

_____

_____

_____

_____

Chapter 4

Unlocking Your Potential

Unlocking Your Potential Notes

---

1. Unlocking Your Potential

Your self-confidence can affect your emotions and mental state in many ways, including your capacity to think straight and be rational. It can impair your system of beliefs, thereby causing self-doubt, including how you perceive yourself and how you interpret other people's behaviour and attitude towards you.

You can become vulnerable, become a target and be taken advantage of because you are not assertive enough to feel empowered and therefore at risk of sexual and financial exploitation. Because your emotions are all over the place, you feel unloved, making you crave for attention; what you often get though is the wrong attention.

How many people do you know that lack confidence and self-esteem and will partner up with anyone that will offer them attention, which has led to sexual, financial, and, in some cases, domestic abuse?

Lack of self-confidence can be caused by the work environment, or past experiences, such as respective childhood, relationships, and personal life in one's home environment. This compounded with lack of support in the work environment, feeling of underachieving, self-doubt, such as not having the necessary skills, knowledge, or expertise in your job, and lack of support from your manager or you team can leave a sense of abandonment. When you lack confidence, it can spill over to other aspects of your personal life.

There are times when your confidence can drop so low that it can completely cause you to become confused, irritable, or aggressive towards yourself and others. You may experience the feeling of not wanting to get out of bed to face the day, often proceeded with depression. You may even experience a feeling of not belonging or think that you don't fit in, labelling yourself, and experiencing self-talk such as "I can't" rather than "I can".

2. Self-Belief

Lack of self-belief is the feeling that you get when you think you are not good enough, not worthy, utterly useless, self-blaming, or blaming others for the way you feel. Your energy level becomes so low that it affects the amount of energy you have to do anything. To the extent that having a bath, getting dressed, going out, meeting up with friends may appear too much and you don't want to be in company with anyone.

Lack of self-belief can cause you to spiral into a negative state of mind to the extent that it takes over your life and induces anxiety, as well as other physical, psychological, and emotional conditions such as constipation, digestive problems, and a general feeling of malaise, which can be self-perpetuating and cause additional health problems.

Due to the pain being experienced, some individuals may, seek the use alcohol or engaging in self-harming behaviour to alleviate the pain and psychological discomfort. All of which will require different levels of intervention such as a medical practitioner or therapeutic intervention such as counselling, mindfulness, yoga, and meditation.

3. *Values*

We all have values that define who we are and what we stand for; however, our values can be eroded in our profession, due to policies, new ways of working etc., which are influenced by finite resources within human resources and appropriate equipment.

This, however, is rarely in the best interest of the client. You are sometimes put in a position to breach the very professional code of practice you had sworn to uphold. For example, I struggled as a nurse in a unit for the elderly in ensuring that all my clients had underwear on. This was done to promote and maintain their dignity. As a child, I was taught this value. As a social worker, you come across clients in their homes that require more than 15 minutes homecare, so that they can be properly washed, groomed, and be provided with time to have their breakfast.

I felt absolutely tormented with the feeling that I had not provided a good service, thus undermining my own values as a professional regarding promoting the client's dignity.

Unlocking Your Potential

As a professional, you can often be put in a situation where your values and beliefs are eroded as well as struggling to deal with the complex issues surrounding care provision, and attempting to find ways in changing the situation.

Sometimes, when you try and change a situation, you can be perceived as an idealist or a trouble maker. Maybe it is because there are some who are sucked into the system, become blind, or they compromise their own values and beliefs to fit into the system.

You can choose to either be sucked in by the system or make what little change you can, knowing that there will be challenges. Be prepared to meet those challenges head on, knowing that there are consequences.

Professionals are compelled to compromise their professional code of practice, ethics and values, mostly due to poor policies and lack of resources to provide the quality of care required for the most vulnerable. Professionals, as a result, are left with very little control. It is often the reason why so many professionals

Self-Appraisal

abandon their profession entirely and channel their passion elsewhere, thus becoming the broken professional.

Model:

Five Steps to Professional Transformation Wheel:

My Value Tool Kit.

5.What can I offer to others?

1.Who Am I?
Self-Awareness

4.What is My Passion?

2.Who/What do I want to Become?

3.What are my Values?

4. Self-Awareness: Who Am I? Who do I want to Become?

4.1 Describe yourself, and ask others to describe what they recognise about you. You must be willing to hear both negative and positive feedback.

_____

_____

_____

_____

_____

_____

4.2 When you have completed this task, read out what you have written about yourself and read what others have said about you. Is there some congruence in what has been said about you?

_____

_____

_____

4.3 Does it actually matter what people say about you?

_____

_____

4.4 What emotions do you get when you receive feedback?

Write down your perception of the feedback you have received and how it made you feel.

_____

_____

_____

_____

After making your list, identify which of those characteristics will be beneficial to you in moving forward as an individual, learner and professional.

- Are there any areas you wish to improve?
- Why?

Unlocking Your Potential

We have all have the capacity to change our behaviour in a way that's going to be beneficial to ourselves and to others. We can choose to laugh, cry, hate, love, resent, envy, self-criticise as well as provide criticism to others, show affection and disempower or empower through verbal and non-verbal communication. Do we not?

Having undertaken the first task, select from the list those qualities that you consider beneficial to yourself

4.5 How have these qualities contributed to your relationship with others?

Fill in on the columns and in each column write down 'Positive' and 'Negative': What emotions do you associate with those feelings?

Self-Appraisal

					Positive
					Feelings
					Negative
					Feelings

4.6 Ask yourself this:

4.6.1 Where do these feelings/emotions come from?

_____

_____

4.6.2 Which of those feelings/emotions do I want for the rest of my life?

_____

_____

4.7 Write down the qualities you want to take forward and the feelings/emotions you want to feel.

_____

_____

_____

_____

_____

_____

Self-Appraisal

What are my Values and Beliefs?

Our values and beliefs influence our behaviour and communication with others.

Write down your values and the behaviour you perceive as being associated with your Values and Beliefs. Where did they come from?

_____

_____

_____

_____

_____

Story

When a colleague of mine made some remarks about my communication style, my answer was simply—I love People! Would I have said that years ago—No! I did not possess the confidence to say those words.

Why? Because it was not 'cool' to say that you love people; in fact, as a professional, if you want to sincerely help others, the first thing you want to do is free yourself from any judgemental thinking and try to establish mutual respect in order to build effective rapport and empathy to help your client.

- What is My Passion?

  _____

  _____

- What can I offer to others?

  _____

  _____

- Reflect on your Values and Beliefs and how have been challenged?

  _____

  _____

- How did you resolve your situation?

  _____

  _____

Self-Appraisal

- What were the lessons that you learnt from your experience?

_____

_____

_____

_____

What are your beliefs and Values on the following:

- Spirituality

_____

- Family

_____

- Honesty

_____

- Health

_____

Unlocking Your Potential

- Equality

  _____

- Communities

  _____

- Relationships

  _____

- Professional Practice

  _____

- Children

  _____

- Elderly

  _____

- Men

  _____

- Women

  _____

Self-Appraisal

- LGBT — (Lesbian, Gay, Bisexual and Transvestite)

_____

- Disabled

_____

- Marriage

_____

- Caring

_____

- Divorce

_____

- Single Parents

_____

- Abuse

_____

- Criminals

_____

Unlocking Your Potential

- Politicians

  _____

- Rich

  _____

- Poor

  _____

- Social Class

  _____

- Legislation

  _____

- Teamwork

  _____

- Friendship

  _____

- Sexuality

  _____

Self-Appraisal

- Politics

  _____

- Immigrants

  _____

- Gangs

  _____

- Race

  _____

- Poverty

  _____

- Wealth

  _____

To get to the next level of self-fulfilment, you must align your values to your goals and aspirations, without knowing what your core values are and what drives them. How you respond to them when challenged will influence your behaviour and can make you more confident in managing your own emotions.

Your values can or may determine what type of occupation you continue to work in, and areas you wish to explore, people you want to associate with, such as what type of professionals, including friends, colleagues, and those you want to serve. However, one should not become a slave to the course at the expense of one's physical, emotional and psychological health which can unfortunately lead to emotional burnout.

My own values have influenced my career path and my passion for serving those I perceive as having no voice: the elderly, disabled, family carers, women, and children.

"Courage doesn't always roar. Sometimes courage is the little voice at the end of the day that says I'll try again tomorrow."
—Mary Anne Radmacher

Self-Appraisal

Notes

_____

_____

_____

_____

_____

_____

_____

_____

_____

_____

_____

_____

_____

_____

Chapter 5

Leveraging Self in the Economy

Leveraging Self in the Economy Notes

---

1. Judgmental vs Non-Judgmental

Your values and beliefs can predict your attitude and behaviour towards another individual or a given situation. These are, ultimately, based on your experiences. Your response to an individual or situation may become automatic because of similar experiences. Often, it may feel that your response can a defense when feeling threatened, fear of loss of personal control, or may even reflect your own inadequacies.

Therefore, when you want to go through the process of transforming self-appraising your own attitudes can free up your mind and prevent distortion. Hence, facing challenges positively without causing you to be judgemental and can open up even more opportunities in serving others that you may not have perceived was possible for you.

Continuous self-appraisal provides the opportunity for reinventing yourself, being more flexible, adapting to change, and increases your personal profile and communication with the diversity of individuals and potential in serving more people.

2. *Story*

As the single assessment project manager for Bedfordshire Health Authority, part of my role was to bring nurses and social workers together to develop the health authorities (Single Assessment Process National Framework for Older People: Section 3).

The first meeting I organised focused on getting social workers and nurses to work together. At the meeting, nurses sat on one table, and social workers sat on another table; unfortunately, neither profession saw the value nor potential to learn from each other, which would ultimately improve communication between them. In fact, they saw the process as a threat to their own professional practice and position.

The nurses and social workers were judge-mental about each other profession and obviously felt threatened, which interfered with professional practice and customer care. Having observed and experienced the situation and the impact it had on the proposed collaboration. I saw the disconnect lay in the difference in professional practice, culture, and communication styles.

I self-appraised my own professional experience and what I could do to be more effective in working across health and social care and embarked on qualifying as a social worker. This is an example of taking action in developing my skills and knowledge.

Having already qualified as a registered nurse, I saw an opportunity for self- development, and that enabled me to have the capacity in working across health and social care sector.

- What positive and negative experiences have you had when working with other professionals?

_____

_____

_____

Self-Appraisal

- What was the impact on your clients?

  _____

  _____

  _____

  _____

- And how did it make you feel?

  _____

  _____

  _____

  _____

- What impact did it have on how you delivered your service?

  _____

  _____

  _____

  _____

  _____

3. *Building On Your Potential: Procrastinating for What!*

In 1994, while working for Bedfordshire Health in commissioning, I presented the business case and strategic framework for integrating health and social care.

My presentation demonstrated ways of involving health, police, social services, community representatives and consumers in influencing service design and quality.

Prior to the board meeting, I discussed the proposal with the director, and he said to me, "Valma, it will never happen". However, I went ahead and presented the case.

Today, partnership, collaboration, and integration are key to collaborative working for improving and promoting seamless services.

This experience demonstrated to me that I had the capacity to be a visionary and the ability to think laterally, which had opened up additional opportunities such as developing and managing consultation and partnership initiatives. The lesson from this experience is to never give up on your idea or your passion!

- How do you think being judgmental can affect your relationship with professionals?

  _____

  _____

  _____

- How do you think being Judgmental can affect those you want to serve?

  _____

  _____

  _____

- What has been your key achievement for influencing professional or organisational change?

  _____

  _____

  _____

4. Self-Investment

Self-appraisal is also about being prepared to invest in your personal development. Often people wait for their employer to invest in their professional development. The current climate of austere employers can be tough and they do not provide training for their employees as they used to back in the days.

In fact, professional training has steadily declined due to lack of resources and funding. As an employee, it is likely that you have to invest in your own training, and if you do request for your employer to pay, you really have to put forward a compelling case and really consider your future in that organisation. Employers will not invest in education and training unless they are certain you will remain within the organisation. The reality is, why would they want to invest in you if you plan on taking their investment elsewhere! Not a chance!

Therefore, it is in your best interest to invest in yourself instead of waiting for your employers to do it? Waiting around for someone to act on your behalf puts shackles on you and distracts you from your purpose. It can also trap you and diminish your potential for personal and professional development and further hamper your progress and monetary value to the organisation and self.

Chapter 6

Alternative Learning Strategies

Alternative Learning Strategies Notes

_____

_____

_____

_____

_____

_____

_____

_____

_____

_____

_____

_____

_____

_____

_____

1. Re-Think Your Learning Strategy

The traditional route to accessing education and learning opportunities has changed considerably over the years. Established institutions such as Colleges and Universities that were recognised as the only means to acquire qualifications are no longer considered as the only route to gaining skills and knowledge.

The rise and ever-increasing access to e training has made it easier to gain accredited qualification. E-learning courses can be accessed more easily all over the world as long you have an access to a computer, internet, and you are motivated.

2. Individualise Learning

There is a recognisable growth in individuals using their accumulation of knowledge, expertise, professional experience, and sharing the information to the masses as a means of generating income.

Self-Appraisal

Some individuals may not have had formal education or have qualifications, but due to their confidence in their expertise create opportunities for sharing their knowledge, such as becoming a public speaker or trainer. Others are using their experience in the field that they are already teaching in such as technology, marketing, social media, coaching, nutrition, counselling and practitioners and have drawn on their own experience and created their own unique profile and branding as experts.

Individuals have taken the opportunity to share their knowledge through a variety of channels, such as workshops, seminars, podcast, books, including YouTube and social media, thus transforming themselves as international and global public speakers with the potential to generate an even bigger income.

Surprisingly, when reflecting on and observing the phenomena of motivational speaking, one can argue that it stems from the church, which I perceive started in the Pentecostal church, where a pastor attempts to capture the souls of the congregation by using emotive language and storytelling to create and get the emotional response they want. Comedians also use this approach, which is now firmly embedded in motivational seminars. However, more emphasis is placed on tapping into the cognitive, psychological, and emotional component of human behaviour.

3. Learning from the Experts

The current trend in the acquisition of learning is for aspiring speakers to package their knowledge, experience, and skills in their chosen field, write a book, and use their book as a mechanism for self-promotion, which has enabled some to become successful entrepreneurs in their field. These include Tony Robbins, Brain Tracy, Oprah Winfrey, and, more recently, Vishal Morjaria to name a few.

4. Self-Directed Learning

Writing a book is now acclaimed as the most effective and efficient approach to generating an interest about self. The ability to draw from one's experience and write about it is phenomenal. Sharing what you have learnt from and along with others is empowering. I have certainly found it amazing when a number of people who stand in a queue patiently waiting to purchase a book and have a word with the author and an opportunity to raise their profile as an expert. I remember waiting in queue to get my book signed by Ruby Max and have my picture taken with her—how amazing that was!

By writing a book, not only are you putting yourself out there as an expert, letting people know who you are and what you do, but you are also sharing your accumulation and wealth of knowledge, wisdom, skills, expertise, experience, and reclaiming back the investment you made into your career and personal development. Yes! It is payback time, and now you are taking control over your career choice and your monetary value.

How often have you had a good idea for improving a product or service, and then went off to share it with your organisation.

They either discarded or took ownership of your idea and then have it discussed and dissected at a management meeting before it's finally implemented.

- Did you receive any recognition for it though?
- Either a raise or a promotion?
- Were you recognised at all?

Yes! This has happened to me and many other professionals; in some cases, you are not given any opportunity to have an input or be engaged in the process, or your manager takes your idea and represent it as theirs.

- Ever been in that situation?

Maybe your idea was given to someone else to develop, and they got the recognition afterwards.

- Is this plagiarism?

How do you ensure that you get recognition for your ideas, expertise, and talent? Write a book! And let people know!

Self-Appraisal

Notes

_____

_____

_____

_____

_____

_____

_____

_____

_____

_____

_____

_____

_____

Chapter 7

Creating Synergy

Creating Synergy Notes

Who can complement my skills and shortfalls.

_____

_____

_____

_____

_____

_____

_____

_____

_____

_____

_____

_____

1. Your Strength

Your strength is your accumulation of knowledge, skills, and experience in your career through investing in training and the willingness and capacity to share your expertise with likeminded professionals and people who want to learn from you. An important aspect of your strength ought to be about planning how to continuously grow your experience, knowledge and expertise, in order to stay up to date.

2. Continuous Professional Development

Continuous professional development is the key phrase and is now recognised as an essential part of ensuring employees and, subsequently, organisations are at the top of their professional game.

There are now more opportunities to link in and access social networks platforms where one can meet like-minded professionals who seek to share and gather information to update themselves on new trends and practices or equally to identify job opportunities through networking.

3. *What Social Networks Can Do for You*

Business networks and professional networks such as "I Am" are aimed at bringing people together to provide means for someone to gain employment in their dream job. Just imagine being at a social network or event where you come across a senior manager or Director—just being in their presence, you have already established contact with a prospective employer.

You have an opportunity to talk to them, which can give you an opening to fish for a potential job interview. You never know; the interaction may be what leads you to your next job.

4. Why Keep Job Description and Job Specification

When you apply for a job, you are given a job description; you leave a job and are given another job description.

- So, what do you do with your job description after you have left an employer?

- Do you file it or throw it into the bin?

I guess if you had a poor relationship with the employer, you would not want to keep that job description in your possession. One, because you may have had an unamicable departure from the organisation, such as being dismissed, sacked or left the employment due to being subject to bullying, discrimination or simply because your health deteriorated.

Therefore, you may well wish to discard any information or any connection you had with that employer.

How often when you write a new CV or apply for a job have you used information from previous job descriptions? I have recognised the value in keeping job descriptions and job specifications. Having reflected on my approach in writing applications by attempting to remember the details of my previous job to match the specifications of a current job, you can fail to remember or re-call important features of a previous job.

Chapter 8

Unleashing the Power Within

Unleashing the Power Within Notes

A job description and job specification are a record of your role and responsibilities as a professional. Some would say that it is a paper exercise, because the work you actually did is not reflected in your job description.

However, we often find that you are given roles and responsibilities that are different to your job title or you have been given additional roles and responsibilities, which can leave you feeling dejected and insecure about your role. However, bearing in mind that you have a job description. Did you ever consider adding to your job description those additional tasks that you were expected to do? How have you used your job descriptions?

Building your Profile

Your professional profile is integral to your personal growth, just as it is with your profile on any social media avenue such as LinkedIn. How you represent yourself to the media is important. You will need to ensure that you send the right image to both professionals, consumers, clients, and prospect business partners.

Therefore reviewing, updating, and building your profile is crucial to being taken seriously and maintaining your professional integrity.

Your profile should reflect you personality, who you are, what you do, and should include a brief career history, interests, achievements, roles and responsibilities, education, your passion, and any specific areas you are interested in, and why people should contact you or want to get to know you.

Facebook

You may be wondering how I let others know what I do, what my areas of expertise are, how I have contributed to influencing positive changes, and bringing value to servicing users' life. First, you have to feel comfortable promoting yourself, so shying away from "self-importance" is not a sin, even though others may make you feel awkward about promoting yourself. So just ignore them if you think you're the best in your field, and you can contribute to improving people's lives. However, you do have to prove it — what testimonials have you received to substantiate your worth and value, what are your credentials, who have said what about you.

Your professional integrity matters to you and others — so start collecting testimonials, start sharing your story, start valuing your worth.

Often, employers fail to recognise the talent of staff, or they are selective; no doubt, you have come across moments where, all of a sudden, you hear someone has been promoted or seconded or received a pay raise, and you are still waiting, irrespective of the contribution you have made. Don't wait for anyone to recognise your talent! You recognise your talent and worth and find other mechanisms for promoting yourself.

- LinkedIn has provided an opportunity for professionals to reach out to other professionals to share good practice and networking opportunities.

Self-Appraisal

Having you considered improving your skills in using social media. Well, I recognise that I was not using social media to move my career forward and decided to embark on a course with Andy Stott. He is an amazing trainer on how to use social media to promote yourself and network; check out his website.

www.bigbusinessevents.co.uk

Self–Appraisal

There are several tools that you can use for self-appraisal, some tools that are used for specific areas can also be used alongside the self-appraisal tool kit. The Wheel of Life, Maslow Hierarchy of Needs, Swot and Pest Analysis, are some of the tools that can be used to self-appraise.

Professional Learning Communities

As a member of a registered body, it is expected that individuals provide evidence of continuous professional practice to ensure that their practices meet the required standard to enable individuals to remain on professional register.

Therefore, you need to embrace any learning opportunity you get that will provide you with the evidence of learning. It relies on you as a professional to identify your training needs as part of the appraisal process, which means that you need to be vigilant and diligent in ensuring that you can access the required training.

According to Law and Glover (1996), they stated that organisations that managed their employee professional development training. Created a supportive environment in which staff feel motivated to learn. They identified the following five factors that contribute to this:

- Effective flow of management information
- Effective and transparent planning process
- Define allocation of resources and aims and objectives of the training

Self-Appraisal

- Effective evaluation systems for monitoring training outcomes
- Effective clear mechanism in which professionals can access peer support and share information

Chapter 9

Scanning Your Environment

Scanning Your Environment Notes

_____

_____

_____

_____

_____

_____

_____

_____

_____

_____

_____

_____

_____

Frameworks that can be applied to identify opportunities for personal and professional growth, and monetise your capabilities.

- **P: Political**
- **E: Economic**
- **S: Social**
- **T: Technological**

1. Political

- What are the current political issues that are informing your profession about their sustainability?

_____

_____

_____

- Does the government provide more funding in your area of expertise?

_____

_____

_____

- Are they recruiting more people in your area of expertise?

  _____

  _____

  _____

- Are there new policies about what the future services will be and the role of professionals?

  _____

  _____

  _____

2. *Economic*

- Are you passionate about helping people and improving people's lives?

  _____

  _____

  _____

Scanning Your Environment

- Are there opportunities in which you can contribute to the economic wellbeing of the society by offering better services than others?

  _____

  _____

  _____

- Are you aware of any potential opportunities that you as a professional can influence?

  _____

  _____

  _____

- Do you have information on how to present a business case for accessing funding or resources, such as government grants?

  _____

  _____

  _____

- Are the issues regional, local, international, global?

  _____

  _____

- What are the emerging gaps in your sector?

  _____

  _____

  _____

  _____

  _____

  _____

3. Social

Underlying social issues such as health, housing, unemployment, mental health, parenting, and so on. These are all social factors that can create opportunities for you to use your expertise, knowledge, and skills within the community.

For example, being aware of local and national policies, funding opportunities aligned with local health and social care plans, or the increase in mental health problems in young people, families, and children. Other sources of income include commissioning services, becoming an expert public speaker in the field or establishing a charity to serve others.

Organisations such as Women's Aid, Carers Trust, residential homes for the elderly and disabled, children's homes, established primarily by professionals creating their own employment or enterprise, and so on.

4. Technical

Learning is now driven by employees accessing online training, some of which may not be an appropriate mechanism for you to be able to really apply in practice, due to different training formats.

An example is online equal-opportunity training and abuse. Although, it may work out more cheaply for employers.

Self-Appraisal

Face-to-face interaction and opportunities for staff to engage more fully in the subject matter is still lacking. Staff lack encouragement to share their experiences, peer training etc.

Therefore, the use of case studies and role play can enable staff to engage more effectively in the learning process, rather than sit looking at a computer screen.

Chapter 10

SWOT

SWOT Notes

_____

_____

_____

_____

_____

_____

_____

_____

_____

_____

_____

_____

_____

_____

SWOT Analysis Tool

S: **Strengths**

W: **Weaknesses or as I prefer to say Potential for development**

O: **Opportunity**

T: **Threats**

1. Strengths

You can apply the Self-Appraisal Tool Kit to identify your strengths. Reflect back on your achievements and successes during your whole employment to establish what your strengths are.

When identifying your strengths, you can also use additional support material, such as YouTube tutorials, attending and networking seminars, and specialist peer support social networks, some of which are free and are highly informative and motivational. Also, they provide an opportunity to find potential business associates or recruitment specialists seeking out potential recruits. You can learn new skills, such as business management, public speaking, and providing social and learning support.

2. *Weaknesses or as I prefer to say Potential for Development*

Through the Self-Appraisal Tool Kit, you will no doubt identify areas that you need to develop or find that you do not yet have sufficient practical experience to feel confident to apply those skills. However, you can bring those up to speed in many ways and become a more rounded person in your professional career.

Often it is not that we have a weakness, which I personally think is associated with negative thinking—I prefer to simply call it gaps in practice and knowledge.

Once you recognise these gaps in practice and knowledge, you can find practical ways to improve your performance. YouTube is a good place to start to identify what you need to learn specifically, if you need to acquire a qualification and at what level. You can also check local colleges and universities; some universities, such as Northampton, offer two-year degrees rather than courses spanning three years or more, education, and getting bums on seats is currently becoming a competitive market. This is alongside individuals' access to specific training on the internet, some of which are reasonably priced.

You may even consider attending local social networks as a means of finding out what is available in the local social networking learning community.

3. Opportunities

As with the Pest Analysis model, founded by Frances, J. Aguilar in 1964, created as a macro environmental analysing tool for scanning business environments, I have found it to be extremely useful when applied to monitor a person's daily life such as career, family, and business. You are encouraged to explore local information about local business opportunities, resources to help small businesses such as grants, free training, and grant availability for special projects.

Obviously, you will have to do your own donkey work, because what you seek you will find; you can find even more information with just enquiring about it from someone else — one question leads to another, so by the time you have finished, you will have a wealth of information to make an informed decision or realise — I NEED MORE!

4. Threats

You may even want to identify through self-appraisal what factors may interfere with your personal and professional development, such as finance; or have you been recently made redundant, or could you invest some of the funds into your training?

Have you worked out what training you will need to ensure that you have the necessary skills and qualifications?

SWOT

Gathering information from your job description and getting testimonials could effectively put you a step above your competitors.

Getting expert advice and information from professional bodies is also a useful tool for getting an insight about changes in your profession so that you can make an informed decision, whether you have the necessary transferable skills to transform and take on another career path.

Self-Appraisal

Notes

_____

_____

_____

_____

_____

_____

_____

_____

_____

_____

_____

_____

_____

Chapter 11

Create the Life
You Want

Create the Life You Want Notes

_____

_____

_____

_____

_____

_____

_____

_____

_____

_____

_____

_____

_____

_____

Changing for a Purpose

- Why Change?

  _____

  _____

- Why do you need to change?

  _____

  _____

- Who is the Change for?

  _____

  _____

These are some of the questions you have to ask yourself in order to establish the identity you want and to create your brand. You might say, "Why do I need to change?" Changing means that you can be congruent with your values and beliefs.

If your values and beliefs do not sit comfortable with who you want to be, it can cause internal conflict and turmoil, to the extent of impacting your emotional, psychological and physical health. It is like being trapped in a body that is not yours. Changing means that you can work from your spirituality and the passion for what you do, in serving others. You might say to yourself:

What does she mean by saying serving others?

We all serve others differently, just being here, wanting to help, supporting, comforting, loving, being sincere, showing compassion and empathy, are all about serving humanity.

Planning Your Exit

Preparation is fundamental when planning your exit and is crucial for the outcome and your future.

Planning a new beginning or starting a new journey is both exciting when you know where you are going and challenging. You may start getting butterflies, perhaps a little bit nauseated and reluctant.

Create the Life You Want

Your exit does not have to be complicated or complex, not if you have made the necessary preparation.

It is rather like planning your holiday…

- When will I do it?

  _____

  _____

- How Do I do it?

  _____

  _____

- What will I get?

  _____

  _____

- What will I see?

  _____

  _____

Self-Appraisal

- What will I feel?

  _____

  _____

- What will I taste?

  _____

  _____

- What will it look like?

  _____

  _____

- What difference will it make?

  _____

  _____

- What will be the key benefits?

  _____

  _____

- Who will it affect?

  _____

  _____

- What is it worth?

  _____

  _____

- How much is it worth?

  _____

  _____

Coaching

Identifying a person you think can support you with your journey or transition is definitely a big boost. It is not about having someone to motivate you, because if you are not motivated yourself, you will not make the necessary changes to get you to your destination.

Self-Appraisal

Consider climbing a rock; yes, it is good to have people cheering you on, but what if there is no one there? Are you going to stand still until someone comes? Your ultimate power within is the driving force for your transition; if you do not have that light, then it will not glow.

Using self-coaching techniques, to self-re-enforce the reasons why you are stepping forward are the most powerful re-enforcement.

- I can and will do this!
- Nothing is stopping me!
- I have the necessary skills, knowledge and expertise!
- I am responsible for my journey!
- Barriers will be there. But I will find an alternative route!
- No! is not the answer!
- I love me, I know nothing is impossible!
- The possibility is me!
- There will be challenges — But I will face them head on!

- This is my purpose!
- I will make a difference!
- I love me enough to know that I can do this with the help of the universe!
- I have a purpose!
- I can do more!
- I will do more!
- I am unstoppable!
- Only I can get in the way of my journey!
- I am working with all that is possible!
- No standing still and no going back!
- My journey is full of joy and surprises!
- I love my journey!

Mentoring

A mentor is someone who can teach or show you how to achieve. This may be someone you like who may inspire you. You may like their style of working, the way that they communicate, how they present themselves, their people skills, their professionalism. This could be someone you directly know in your field or in another professional area.

In passing, you may have observed that others have a particular approach that you would like to develop. Tony Robbins and many others have reported that if you want to achieve find someone in the field and ask them how they do it. However, this is easier said than done. But it is not impossible.

Developing the right habits to help you transform, be successful and achieve the outcome may mean finding someone who can alongside your development shares your journey to create the right environment for your professional or personal development.

For me, the people who inspire me and have the values that I feel most comfortable with are the likes of Madam Teresa, Princess Diane, Martin Luther King, Mahatma Gandhi, Rose Parks, John F. Kennedy, Robert Kennedy, Oprah Winfrey, Abraham Lincoln, Angela Davis, Diane Abbot. These individuals have inspired me and, of course, my beloved mother, Elizabeth Brotherson, for their tenacity and wisdom to wanting to make a difference.

> *"An ounce of practice is worth*
> *more than tons of preaching."*
> —*Mahatma Gandi*

Self-Appraisal

Notes

_____

_____

_____

_____

_____

_____

_____

_____

_____

_____

_____

_____

_____

_____

Chapter 12

Reaching Your Destiny

Reaching Your Destiny Notes

_____

_____

_____

_____

_____

_____

_____

_____

_____

_____

_____

_____

_____

Your Action Plan

Developing your action plan is a perquisite to moving forward, just writing it down get your mind in the right state, creating a new neural mental pathway that will keep you focus should be integrated in your action plan.

In your action plan, you create and write down each step that you will take to get to your destination. It just like planning your journey to a shop, you need to identify how you will get there; this is no different to planning that journey.

You can write your action plan anywhere, you may wish to write in on a sheet of paper and post it somewhere where it is visible, that reminds you what you said you are going to do. Look at your action plan each day, perhaps before you go to bed and when you wake in the morning, so you are utterly focused on your intentions.

Self-Appraisal

Goal Setting

Setting out your goals is key to supporting you in taking action each day. Specifically setting out each goal for each of the activities you want to achieve, should be included in your action plan. I normally would use a three-step goal-planning template, which includes the goals I want to achieve:

- Write down three specific steps I need to undertake to achieve the goal.

    Step 1–

    _____

    _____

    Step 2–

    _____

    _____

    Step 3–

    _____

    _____

Reaching Your Destiny

- What would I see when I have achieved the goal for each step?

  Step 1–

  _____

  _____

  Step 2–

  _____

  _____

  Step 3–

  _____

  _____

- What I would feel when I have achieved the goal for each step.

  Step 1–

  _____

  _____

Self-Appraisal

Step 2–

_____

_____

Step 3–

_____

_____

- What difference it has made to myself and significant others?

_____

_____

Meditation

Some individuals have found meditation beneficial in helping them to clear their mind and enable them to focus. Often, we have so much information going on in our minds that it can become overwhelming and we can get lost in the amount of information jumping around in own mind.

The ability to clear the mind and only focus on the intentions of now! Is extremely important and beneficial in helping to focus, clearly your mind how and supporting you to implement the actions you want to take to begin your purpose.

Sometimes this may be about taking the opportunity to go for a walk, sitting in silence to gather your thoughts or just having a coffee at a local café shop, or finding a quiet space. Just to think and plan.

Visualisation

Some have found that using visualisation as an approach for helping them to have some internal and external vision on what they what to achieve.

Here are some approaches that can be used.

Using meditation to set out the goals you want to achieve by thinking about your goals and meditating on them

Self-Appraisal

Use a vision board; collect photographic images of what you want and place them on a board to visually track and guide your journey. For example, there may be something or things that you physically want, such as a specific house. Get a picture of the house or type of house you want and place it on your vision board.

Thoughts and Barriers that Can Create Barriers to your pathway and future...

- Using your imagination to create your reality
- Things that you can do to reduce your possibilities in achieving what you want
- Making negative judgements about others
- Hate and anger in your energy
- Self-sabotaging
- Allowing others to disempower you
- Disrespecting and disempowering others
- Self-hatred

- Meanness and lack of Kindness
- Ungratefulness
- Inability to respect differences
- Lack of planning
- Lack of motivation
- Inability to Focus
- Procrastination
- Fear and Rejection
- Not taking care of your mental, physical, emotional and psychological health
- Not taking care of your finance or poor financial planning
- Lack of sincerity
- Failure to Plan and Take Action.

Taking the steps into Consultancy

Taking the first step into developing yourself as an expert in your field and practice can be the most exciting and overwhelming satisfaction you feel — why?

Self-Appraisal

Because you perceive that you know that you have contributed to helping service user improve their life, empowered them to take more control and equally help them to understand the reasons for their circumstances.

Whether it be understanding their problems and developing strategies or tools in which reduce the triggers which can lead to stress, identifying resources, to manage their circumstances in an improved way, contributing to improving their quality of life.

This may include develop service users confidence in navigating health and social care systems in which can contribute to reducing social, health, economic and educational exclusion, prevent a deterioration in their mental health and well-being, accessing the right services and promoting their self-advocacy.

Knowing that you have made a difference as a health and social care professional through using your expertise, knowledge, experience, working with other professionals, involving other agencies, and identifying appropriate partners that can also contribute positively contribute to achieving a positive outcome for the service user is most rewarding.

However, often working in bureaucratic organisations that have their own goals, targets and performance indicators, not knowing where to get resources or professional boundaries and in fighting between professionals as to "whose job it is" professional conflict — can often hold professionals back, including the service for the client which can make a difference to their circumstances and quality of life.

How often have you come across agencies swabbing about whose role it is, who funds the service leaving the client in the middle delaying access to services, creating uncertainty and insecurity for the professional and client. This affects the service user's confidence with the professional and institution, leaving both parties frustrated. Inevitably, these can affect professional relationships with the client, family carers and other agencies and, most importantly, the client's relationship with the professional.

Self-Appraisal

Taking the first steps as a professional into consultancy, can be most rewarding when you have more control on how you work with the client, without having to think how many levels do I have to go through for a decision to be made for the client. In the consultant capacity who have more flexibility in identifying more options for helping the client.

Therefore, to embark on the status as a professional consultant arguable it is important that you either know who the decision makers are or make enquire to find out the information and build up rapport with other professionals.

I tend to use the phrase "No Man is an Island", a quote by English poet **John Donne** (1572-1631) who states that human beings do badly when they individualise their existence and think that they can entirely exist alone, without others, or an individual or group in their life; he argues that one needs to co-exist and be part of a community in order to thrive. So often we forget that our wins include those individuals who may have provided information, resource, encouragement, empowerment which provide the capacity to achieve that goal or successful you perceive you alone achieved. So don't forget to thank those that had contributed to your success, even the smallest contribution desires a thank you!

"Each man is an island unto himself. But though a sea of difference may divide us, an entire world of commonality lies beneath."

—James Rozoff

Nelson Mandela quotes

"Education is the most powerful weapon which you can use to change the world."

"It always seems impossible until it's done."

"After climbing a great hill, one only finds that there are many more hills to climb."

www.bing.com/search?q=nelson+mandela+

Self-Appraisal

Professional Survival Mode: Existence and Survival Mode

Existence and Survival Mode: Self-Scoring 7 step Monitoring Tool Kit.

(Self-esteem, self-confidence, & self-worth)
Score from 1- 10
1: Being the lowest score and 10: Being the highest.

1. Low Self Esteem, Self Confidence, & Self Worth	2. Problem Solving: Critical Thinking & Reflection
3. Identify & Define key Issues or Problems	4. Apply Problem Solving Techniques

Explore Meaning of Emotions & Feelings: Mind, Body & Soul

(Physical, psychological, emotional, dietary, nutrition, relationships, love, anger, other...

5. Apply Reflective Practice: Explore Mindfulness, Meditation, Exercise, Spirituality, other...	6. Define Main Problem: Action & Goal to resolve Issue/problem

7. Apply Self-Monitoring (1—10)
Create Your own positive quote & affirmation to build
Self-confidence, self -esteem & Self -worth
Sustainability & Self Preservation
I will... I can... I am... I have...

High Self Confidence and Self Esteem

128

*"Do you want to know who you are?
Don't ask. Act! Action will delineate
and define you."*
— *Thomas Jefferson*

*"What you do makes a difference,
and you have to decide what kind of
difference you want to make."*
— *Jane Goodall*

What are your Values and Beliefs?

Knowing and understanding from where values and belief are generated enables a professional to have an improved understanding of the lives and circumstances of their clients.

Exercise

• Write down your values and beliefs.

_____

_____

Self-Appraisal

- Write down your associated behaviour with your values and beliefs.

  _____

  _____

- How has your values and beliefs influence your style in caring?

  _____

  _____

  _____

- How has your values and beliefs influence your practice?

  _____

  _____

  _____

- Has self-appraisal of your values and beliefs shifted? Yes / No

  _____

  _____

  _____

- If yes, what has shifted?

_____

_____

_____

_____

_____

Story

When I a comment was made to me by a colleague about my communication style, that they said is calming. I was not aware of the impact it had on others, until I reflected on my interaction with clients.

On one occasion, whilst in an accident and emergency service, a client was shouting his head off. I quietly walked behind the cubicle screen, said hello, and asked him how he was, not realising that my interaction had stopped his shouting.

Honestly, I do not think it was my voice, more so that I gave attention to the patient.

However, at the time in answering my colleagues question, I had simply said, "I love people!" Would I have said that years ago? No!

Some people would I thought I was crazy; furthermore, I did not have the confidence to say that, because it was not perceived to be cool to say you love people.

In fact, saying you "love people" would have been perceived as if you think you are someone special, so I never said it. However, I have learnt what makes me happy and how I want to serve and be of value to those I come into contact with, it is only because I understand where my values and beliefs come from and how they were formed. Hence, as a professional, if you want to sincerely help others, know yourself.

In our profession, we are taught as part of our values that we should be nonjudgemental, have mutual respect, and treat others with dignity. However, these principles are important if you wish to develop and establish effective rapport and empathy with your client.

"Love is the absence of judgment."
— Dalai Lama XIV

What can I offer to others?

Quote:

"You must be the change you want to see in the world."

"As human beings, our greatness lies not so much in being able to remake the world— that is the myth of the atomic age—as in being able to remake ourselves."

—Mahatma Gandhi.

What is my Passion?

First, to enjoy life, you have to have passion about something that turns you on, excites, motivates, and creates such enthusiasm that your colleagues are envious about what is putting that smile on your face — to the extent that they want to wipe that smile off your face and de-stable you or even disempower you.

You know what I mean; some individual such as a friend, colleague, or manager will want to trip you up, bring you down, see you fall because they do not understand what makes you smile or why you are always positive. I guess you come across them! Well, I have too — but I resist being put into a negative state because if it is not beneficial to my client or me. As you know how you feel is reflected outwardly, so if I am in a negative state — what would my communication be like with myself and others.

How would it affect my personal energy state and my motivation? Yes, being in a negative state change the way you think, behaviour interact, and live your life. I have come across professionals that every word that came out of their mouth was negative, negative about their client, negative about a member of staff, negative about a friend, relative or colleague.

So how do you manage those negative vibes that present themselves and reduce your power to live, be motivated, be happy, be creative, be caring, be loving, be giving, and be grateful for the gifts, wisdom, and talents given to you.

When you are passionate about something that excites you to the extent that you feel the passion in your bones and soul and exhibit it in your behaviour and communication with others. It can be overwhelming to those observing. So, you have to tell them why you are passionate, why you are excited, because if you do not tell them they form their own opinions about you. Don't be afraid to say I am passionate about helping others.

"Being passionate is a state of mind that acts on your internal system and your emotions"

"Be passionate about the things that matters to you, as long as it does not hurt you or others and your intent is sincere and is done in good faith and love of others. Passion is the driver to your success."
—Valma

Self-Appraisal

*"Our doubts are traitors, and make us
lose the good we oft might win,
by fearing to attempt."*
—William Shakespeare

Chapter 13

Negative vs Positive Energy

Negative vs Positive Energy Notes

_____

_____

_____

_____

_____

_____

_____

_____

_____

_____

_____

_____

_____

What can I offer to others?

Every human being has something that they can offer, learn, give, and contribute including the opportunity to inspire others.

- Why do we go into a specific profession? How many times have you been asked this question?

- Why did you choose your profession — some would instantly give their reasons, whilst others take time to reply.

Those who provided their reasons indicated that they to help others, such as providing comfort, compassion in times of distress like a nurse, therapist, or to heal someone in the role of a doctor or therapist, and to help to resolve problems within their capacity as a social worker.

Some wanted to share and teach expertise in the capacity as a teacher or lecturer. Many indicated that, ultimately, it was about interacting with people. Whatever the chosen profession, the idea stems from somewhere. It could be influenced by one's own experience, influenced by others, and their experiences in the profession that there were opportunities in that particular profession; you may have joined your profession due to your circumstances or luck.

Reflecting on my reasons for going into nursing was that my mother wanted to be a nurse, and, at the same time, it provided accommodations and paid training; nursing had been associated with a status .

In fact, I wanted to be a teacher; at the time, it was out of my reach, because I had no accommodations. It was virtually impossible for a Caribbean person to get into a teaching school. Having worked across health and social services, I decided to train as a social worker, and that gave me more flexibility in my career.

Secondly, every human being has a talent; some of us know what that talent is. Others have recognised through observing you; the last person often to recognise that they have a talent is the person that has that talent. Have you come across an individual, and you acknowledged their ability or work? Do they acknowledge your compliment!

Unfortunately, in some cultures, accepting positive compliments such as saying "Thank you" is done with awkwardness or embarrassment.

Have you ever said to someone 'You look great!' What is your instant reaction to saying those words?

Self-Appraisal Analysis Tool Kit

Transformation

There are a number of structures that you can use to develop an action plan that will clearly and concisely organize your goals. Choose a mechanism that best suits you and is clear and practical enough to do what you want it to do. Some will develop a vision that sets out clearly what they want to achieve using pictures, symbols, and cuttings from magazines.

Others will come up with a sheet in which they write down their goals, set out how they aim to achieve them, and the requisite timeframe needed in achieving those goals. The idea is to have something that is visual, that you can monitor on a regular basis to remind you of your goal.

Coaching and Mentoring

Some argue that having a coach or mentor can provide an added value when you explore what you want to achieve. Think of it as a guide in the direction that is most effective in developing your action and implementation plan.

Having a coach also means that you have someone that you are accountable to and will of course question you about your achievements that you had set out to do.

Self-Appraisal

Personal Development Resources Available

- Chamber Of Commerce For Business
- You Tube
- Banks
- Local Authorities
- Experts in Recognised Fields
- Professional Networks such as RCN
- Seminars
- Conferences
- Linked In
- Workshops

Do your research to find what works best for you.

Chapter 14

Negative vs Positive Energy

Negative vs Positive Energy Notes

_____

_____

_____

_____

_____

_____

_____

_____

_____

_____

_____

_____

_____

1. What is negative energy?

My understanding of negative energy is when you have that sense of feeling that you are not deserving of self, and you have very little confidence or no confidence at all. You undermine your own capabilities and allow others to ridicule and disempower you. Your self-worth is always at a base line, and you take crap from other people that does not belong to you. This negativity distorts your natural energy into negative energy that affects the conversation you have with others and self.

I often feel this negative energy in my gut, then my heart, and then my head; it can become self-destructive if you allow it. It takes practice, because there are so many challenges in life and staying in contact with some colleagues, friends, family, your husband, wife, or partner that constantly makes you feel bad about yourself for too long will eventually lead to you becoming their "victim".

Do you wish to have a choice?
Of course, you do!

Self-Appraisal

A story

I was organising a conference when I rang up an organisation that I had volunteered with and informed them that the Minister of State for Health was attending; then I was told, more or less, it will not happen!

Could you imagine if I had allowed that negative communication to get in the way of what I wanted to achieve.

Guess what?
You'll see when you get to page 162
if The Minister had attended.

- Have you experienced this and how did it make you feel?

_____

_____

_____

_____

_____

Negative vs Positive Energy

- Write down all the times someone has said to you something negative that had or could have changed your direction.

  _____

  _____

  _____

  _____

  _____

- How did it make you feel?

  _____

  _____

- What were the emotions you experienced?

  _____

  _____

- What did you see?

  _____

  _____

Self-Appraisal

- What did you feel and where did you feel it?

  _____

  _____

- What experience came back to you?

  _____

  _____

- What did you do with that negativity?

  _____

  _____

- What did you do about how you felt?

  _____

  _____

It is the action we take that determines whether we go forward or stay in the box.

Negative vs Positive Energy

Positive Energy

You may ask, "What is the difference between negative energy and positive energy?" Let me enlighten you! Positive energy is when you feel good and are in a growth mindset (whatever action you take will work out). It determines how your entire body feels; it is like a bubble around you, and whatever negative forces come your way, it bounces off. It is like a spiritual, physical, and emotional protection.

First, you have to love your existence, be grateful for being alive. Have gratitude to that higher being, whatever you may call it; I call it God or the Higher Being. You must have belief that there is something much higher than self and that nothing is impossible if you work at it.

Yes, there are going to be times when you think, 'What is the use!' It is whether you will allow something or someone to get in the way of your dreams. That is the positive energy that will inevitably determine the outcome of your hopes, aspirations, and dreams.

Self-Appraisal

Look at all those who have had major obstacle in their life; Oprah Winfrey, Nelson Mandela, and many others have faced their challenges, but that never stopped them dreaming and hoping. Believing and having the passion to encapsulate the necessary energies that allow them to serve others and self, the core sentiment of "Best Interest to Self and Humanity".

Remember, there will be someone or something that will deliberately get in the way; it is your energy that determines your outcome!

It is your emotions that you internalise which determines how you react what actions you take

If you wish you, can allow your dreams to be someone else 's dream?

So, take control of your dream as long as it is not causing mental, physical and emotional

pain that is self-destructive or destructive to another human soul!

There is a native Caribbean saying "What goes round comes round".

Also, one must beware of their own thoughts about self and others! Whatever you think is what you can get!

Our Deepest Fear

by Marianne Williamson from A Return To Love: Reflections on the Principles of A Course in Miracles

"Our deepest fear is not that we are inadequate. Our deepest fear is that we are powerful beyond measure.

It is our light, not our darkness that most frightens us. We ask ourselves, Who am I to be brilliant, gorgeous, talented, fabulous? Actually, who are you not to be? You are a child of God. Your playing small does not serve the world. There is nothing enlightened about shrinking so that other people won't feel insecure around you. We are all meant to shine, as children do. We were born to make manifest the glory of God that is within us. It's not just in some of us; it's in everyone.

Self-Appraisal

And as we let our own light shine,
we unconsciously give other people
permission to do the same.

As we are liberated from our own fear,
our presence automatically
liberates others."

"Do one thing every day that scares you."
—Eleanor Roosevelt

"Hold fast to dreams, For if dreams die,
Life is a broken-winged bird,
That cannot fly."
—Langston Hughes

"Courage is the most important of all the
virtues because without courage,
you can't practice any other
virtue consistently."
— Maya Angelou

Negative vs Positive Energy

*"It is good to love many things,
for therein lies the true strength,
and whosoever loves much
performs much, and can
accomplish much, and what is done
in love is well done."*
—Vincent Van Gogh

*"The things you do for yourself are gone
when you are gone, but the things
you do for others remain as
your legacy."*
—Kalu Ndukwe Kalu

*Understanding is the first step to
acceptance, and only with acceptance
can there be recovery."*
—J.K. Rowling,
Harry Potter and the Goblet of Fire

Self-Appraisal

"If you treat an individual as he is, he will remain how he is. But if you treat him as if he were what he ought to be and could be, he will become what he ought to be and could be."

— *Johann Wolfgang von Goethe*

"Attitude is a choice. Happiness is a choice. Optimism is a choice. Kindness is a choice. Giving is a choice. Respect is a choice. Whatever choice you make makes you. Choose wisely."

— *Roy T. Bennett, The Light in the Heart*

Chapter 15

Words into Actions

Words into Actions Notes

Build your own personal resources

Exercise—Self-Discovery

Things that you can do to reduce your possibilities in achieving what you want

Stage 1: *Reflect on Words or comments that you perceive have been negative about self?*

For example:

Any words, actions, behaviours, or comments made to you as a child, adult, friend, employee, wife, or husband. You may feel that some of these thoughts can conjure up and bring back painful experience; consider doing this exercise with someone you trust, and with whom you feel safe for self-disclosure. You may wish to meditate before you embark on this exercise to put yourself in the right frame of mind (into a positive state).

_____

_____

Self-Appraisal

Stage 2: Swapping and Changing the Energy

2.1 Making negative judgements self or others: What judgements have you made about yourself:

_____

_____

_____

_____

_____

2.2 Can you change those judgements or comments into constructive comments – or enlist from the negative comments something that can be turned into a positive that will energise the comment.

_____

_____

_____

_____

_____

Self-Appraisal

Stage 3: Self-Improvement

List the things you need to do to change and create the life you want for:

Yourself

_____

_____

_____

_____

_____

_____

Family

_____

_____

_____

_____

_____

_____

Words into Actions

Community

_____

_____

_____

_____

_____

_____

_____

Business

_____

_____

_____

_____

_____

_____

_____

Any others? Please include in the list

_____

_____

_____

_____

_____

Stage 3: Change Maintenance

What are the necessary thoughts that you will have to maintain each second, minute, day, week, month, and year to keep you in a positive state?

_____

_____

_____

_____

_____

What are the things you perceive you will need to do to prevent you self-sabotaging or allowing someone else to sabotage how you feel and what you do each day?

_____

_____

_____

_____

_____

Stage 4: My Spirituality

Reflect on whether you need spirituality in your life. If you do or do not, how do you feel right now! Write down!

_____

_____

_____

_____

_____

Stage 5: Who and what will motivate me?

_____

_____

_____

_____

_____

Stage 6: My Body is My Temple:

How I will care for my mental, physical, emotional, and psychological well-being!?

_____

_____

_____

_____

_____

Words into Actions

Stage 7: My Finance

7.1 How do you feel about money?

_____

_____

_____

_____

_____

7.2 How do you feel about increasing your income and wealth?

_____

_____

_____

_____

_____

_____

Self-Appraisal

7.3 How do you intend on doing it?

_____

_____

_____

_____

_____

_____

_____

Stage 8: My Affirmations

_____

_____

_____

_____

_____

_____

Failure to plan and take action. I have learnt from personal experience that knowing who you are, what you want, recognising and appreciating your talents, thanking the universe, acknowledging that you're not alone, and being willing to serve will keep you happy!

Love yourself; it is so much easier to love others.

Valma

END!

Caroline Dinenage Minister of State for Care and Ministerial Lead for Carers: Department of Health and Social Care Health attended my second National Conference : Health of the Nation: Think Autism! Perspective on Caring for Children and Adults with Autism.

June 11th 2019. Holiday Inn, London.

I am thankful to Caroline Dinenage, MP, in contributing in supporting me achieving my goal.

"Life MOVES WHEN YOU Move It!"
Valma

Printed in Poland
by Amazon Fulfillment
Poland Sp. z o.o., Wrocław

56314751R00116